Mimi Sasso
Amavi, Amo, Amabo

Poetry, Reflections, & Confessions

R. GALLUCCI

Stefano !
Keep a cool store !
Gallucci

DOLCE BOOK PUBLISHING INC.

~ 2006 ~

Mimi Sasso
Amavi, Amo, Amabo

First edition
National Library of Canada Cataloguing in Publication
R. Gallucci
Mimi Sasso
Amavi, Amo, Amabo
www.mimisasso.com

ISBN: 0-9734656-4-6
PRINTED IN CANADA

Dolce Book Publishing Inc.
111 Zenway Boulevard, #30, Vaughan, ON L4H 3H9
905.264.6789 • 1.888.68.DOLCE • www.dolcebookpublishing.ca

This book is dedicated to:
Elena Gallucci, nee De Miglio

The embodiment of the quintessential mother that, "kept the hurt so I would not...".
She was often heard saying, *"iati a scrivere n'a poisia."*
It has taken a lifetime to comprehend the intent of her words.

Acknowledgements
For their unconditional support, faith and trust:

Mario Cortellucci
Ginesia Cortellucci
Eros Gerardi

I thank Andrea Elena Gallucci, blood of my blood, for making me proud of her
in her ability to confront the challenges of life in a positive and mature fashion.

I thank Olivia Carpino for allowing me to challenge myself
in more ways than she could imagine.

I thank Mary, Olga, Carmen, and Gina, my sisters, with whom I share a bond
that transcends, the "scars we took along the way," for a lifetime of unwavering
love and understanding that I feel daily and who remain the lifeline to my sanity.

I thank Santina Carpico, the light saber at my side, that imbues me
with the confidence to explore those darker places in my soul
nonjudgmentally and with whom I embrace serendipity.

Foreword

Poetry is a way that human beings nurture the soul, indeed it is essential to the unfolding of the inner being. This collection of poems is an example of such "inner worships."

The emotional intensity of the images created by this poet, through remembering the influences of culture, family and place, simultaneously provoke, challenge and illuminate.

The places so clearly delineated in this work seem to be less about a physical space and more about the heart of the poet, the soul engaged in the "dance of language," in the embrace and release that comes from insight and just as important "confession."

These poems seem to be about the redemption that comes when image and language meet in the cauldron of the heart and in the imagination of the poet.

The poet interprets his experiences and reconstructs them through poetry. We, in turn, as readers of the text, are invited to recover meaning and reconstruct it for ourselves to make it an educative experience.

There is much pain in this work, there is much anger – indeed, readers might be inclined to "avert their eyes," and yet, the work is not without the mix of insight and yes, hope.

The light for all of us is in the bearing of the soul. This work reminds us that we all need to listen, to gather and name our pain and act responsibly. Like the poet, we need to feel, know, and acknowledge our despair. But, like the poet, we need not stop there.

Like the poet, we are encouraged to move forward into language, into relationship, into community and into life. It is a book worth reading because the sacred cry for unity of the soul weaves its magic web between the lines and holds us in the meditative silence that each word is wrapped in.

As readers, we are drawn into our own sacred stories, our own emotional landscape and our own pain, and in between, the lines meet the poet – let ourselves be seen, read and acknowledged, and, like the poet, set free.

The book ends with a special kind of love poem that carries both the poet and the reader into a place of light, hope and the courage to carry on. It is this hope that helps us break free from our predetermined expectations and takes us to new levels of understanding our own experiences.

Jo-an Collins, Ph.D.
Carmen Maggisano, Ph.D.

Contents

Family

We're not so different

There was too much sorrow

She went to him

It never should have been

It didn't matter

I saw you

He took her

Gentle

Fair

We're not so different

We're not so different
you and you and you
and I
and you___!
The weathered furrows on our brow
reflect
the scars
we took along the way,
to here,
where all that matters most
is hidden...
in a withered smile,
a frozen hand,
the shadow
of_____the life_____
that gave us life
and here
along the way...
we find,
we're not so different
you and you and I
and you and you
and her
and sometimes him!

There was too much sorrow

There was too much sorrow
on her mind
to notice us,
huddled around the kitchen table,
at a memory
that had been
forgotten.
She cried so long
when she heard the news
it was all she could do
to stop herself from going crazy.
We were still too young to understand her agony
but we felt sorry
seeing her pain
and trying hard not to listen to the moaning.
It would take
a lifetime
to fully understand the grief she'd felt
and
as we realized
it never did leave.
We tried to be good those next few days
but youth has its own expectations
and we went about with our own lives
as if nothing really mattered,
and it didn't.
Only when we lost her
did those cries and moans come back to haunt us,
almost as if
they had hidden themselves in a closet,
waiting for the moment
to come and remind us
of the time,
when there was too much sorrow
on her mind
to notice us,
huddled around the kitchen table.

R. Gallucci   ~ 15 ~   Mimi Sasso Amavi, Amo, Amabo

She went to him

She went to him
amid
the olive trees
and figs
and berries
on the vine
that bled the
juice
of ripeness
on her thigh!
Between the passion
and her
new desire
she felt the flesh of dew
and gave her life
to unborn
dreams
and fallen olive trees
and figs
and berries on the vine
that bled her soul
till only unborn
dreams
could fall beneath the
whispers
of the figs
and berries on the vine.

It never should have been

It never should have been
that way.
Her pain too hard
to feel
and furrowed eyes
that told me
it was time.
She knew
and wanted me to know
and kept the hurt
so I would not!
It never should have been
that way!
Kind...
she shed the
light of resigned wisdom
on my life
to make me see
and feel
beyond the knowing eyes
it never should have been
and yet,
it was
and so I wanted her
to know
I knew,
so she would know
it never should have been
that way.

It didn't matter

It didn't matter
much,
to her,
that day.
Her worn-out shoes
survivors
of the countless roads
that led her,
nowhere,
and then to
here,
where there was no more road
and no more pain,
to drag,
along the way
and so...
it didn't really matter,
much,
to her,
to them,
that day.

I saw you

I saw you
                    old man
            beneath the rubble
        of your
            injured mind,
        reaching out
    to cold and withered hands
            that led you
        here,
among the thorns of doubt
and seeds of lost forevers,
that even time
will not
erase
nor memories
subside.
        I saw you
                old man,
your tortured eyes
reflecting the sorrow
of a million aimless days
of twisted dreams
            and loved you still.

I saw you old man.
I saw your desperation
reaching out
and held you to my breast
and cried.

He took her

He took her
then
to fields of golden
sunshine
and daisies on the ground,
promising
the hope
that future
heaps on
future...
and much too kind
to see the
darkness
of the sky
reflected in
his eyes
she sang the song
that lovers sing,
the one I heard
too late
and only promising
the hope
that future
heaps on present fears
I will not
forget the darkness
of the evening sky
reflected in
his eyes.

Gentle

Gentle,
in a strange land.
Alone.
Except for me and you.
Memories of teary eyes waving at the train.
Too late to ever meet again.
No more waves, his cold hand and spirit gone.
A gentle soul,
seeking the strength for you and me,
smiling to ease the pain.
Too proud to fall,
grasping us to her bosom,
that all too soon,
would take her strength and her!
That sweet soul whose hand will wave
no more.

Just me and you
and memories of tired eyes
waving
at the train.

Fair

Fair
she
was
and
something of
a shadow.
She slipped
between
the
silk and cotton
wetness of
a dream
to foreign
eyes
and soft
embraces
of the
hidden kind
that only shadows
find
and dreams
unfurl
beneath the
milky morning dew
and a strange
goodbye.

Generic

Traces

She placed the red rose

The seventh shadow

The soundless spectre

Traces

Traces of butterflies and flowers
over eastern mountain passes,
in lush green fields
of poppies
and hundreds of years
of leftover tears,
loom fondly,
through the lumbering
stillness of time.
Dreams,
interrupted
by slow moving
colourful clouds
in cold dark chambers
ignore the changing passions
of empty moonlit landscapes
as thoughts,
meander and merge,
near the riverbanks
of shimmering waves and soft green grass
that guards all solitudes
through childhood memories
and a maze
of uneasy illusions.

She placed the red rose

She placed
      the red rose
         in a bucket
and
 entered
      the world
         of the insane.
      Napoleon
      was watching
         but he couldn't pull his hand
         out of his vest.
    He was strapped and
         F___ing under the stairwell.
    It was frustrating
     but
       extremely
            liberating.

The seventh shadow

The seventh shadow
          Of the seventh moon
     descended
          like a jackal,
no cloak to hide its face,
no grin to hide its wrath...
          The seventh shadow of the
seventh moon
          passed slowly...
     caressed my pain
and lifted me to Dante's third
          without a call,
     no knock
          to bid its welcome.
The seventh hour
          Of the seventh day
     came quickly,
     descending like
                    a lamb,
               ravaging
                    my soul.

The soundless spectre

The soundless spectre
in my mind
that waits
with anxious smiles
and endless fears
for me to take the road
I should not travel
and when I do
keeping pace
and trying hard to
get my attention.
Will I ever understand
the deeper
complications of my steps?
One sided
it sees only what I
will endure
and..........
tied to me....... soundless,
cannot but
smile the knowing smiles
and shed the
endless tears.

Hometown

It didn't have to happen

The experience

Early mornings

I come from a place

I take refuge

It had been one of the best summers

The bell of Santa Maria Delle Grazie

The midnight breeze

It was quiet in the village

Mimi Sasso

In her delight

It didn't have to happen

It didn't have to happen but it did!
In that remote
and hidden mountain town
that's lost its name,
the peasants worked and toiled
but all for naught.
The years of subjugation, through taxes
war and drought
had worn them
to the bone,
had worn them out.

The French had just arrived
with promises of help
and everyone
revived
their hope
for justice,
peace
and for a better life___
but men are fools
and soon the soldiers,
who were commissioned
in this mountain town,
grew arrogant and wild,
just like the Bourbons
who had come before
and raped,
with no regard,
a girl too young.

It didn't have to happen but it did!
The news
came fast

to all the men
of that poor mountain town
and this was more
than they could
all abide.

At that moment,
in that place and time,
the years of hunger,
degradation, war
and pain
came to an end!

Soon the fourteen French
were dead.
Their arrogance and pride were gone.
It didn't have to happen but it did!
The armies came
to that small mountain town
through orders from that
frail, lame king
and so
began
the bloody massacre
of that small mountain town
and everyone
for all the miles around.
It didn't have to happen but it did!

The devastation and savagery
that was heaped upon this world
is just a note, a sigh,
well hidden in the archives of the mind.

It didn't have to happen but it did!

xperience

The experience was daunting,
                    fraught with hardship.
        Making the trip
        from the small mountain town
                                        to Naples
                                        was already an ordeal,
                    being jammed
                    on a ship
                    used to haul freight
                    was a horror.
Once proud men and women
        subjected to gross inhumanity.
                    Nothing close
                    to what the advertisements
                    declared.
        The sixteen-day voyage
                            found these naïve strangers
                            seasick
                                    for most of the travel.
                                    Many took ill and died.
            No matter,
        there were more where they came from.
Those that did survive
did so
despite
the rations
of salted fish
and potatoes.
        The irony is that
            they were checked
            for disease
            at Halifax
                    and many were sent back.

For those
that remained,
the humiliation and degradation
was something
they did not easily forget.

He cried
when they told him she was leaving,

he remembered the ordeal,
he remembered the sickness and the hunger,
he remembered the pain of leaving his children,
he remembered the loneliness,
he remembered
he remembered
he remembered

and he cried.

Early mornings

Early mornings
were always serene
in that little mountain town.

Birds chirping,
donkeys braying
and roosters
signaling
the arrival of a new day
with a boisterous and proud "chichirichi."

There was no fear of traffic congestion
or timelines
to get to work at a certain hour.

The pace of life was relatively slow
and the women
took their time
getting up,
to prepare for the daily chores,
while waiting for the men
to ready their "ciucciariello"
for the long walk,
to the fields,
where they worked,
tilling the soil
for their crops
and tending to the sheep,
who went their way,
errantly,
without discourse
and without
a care.

I come from a place

I come from a place
that's just
south of nowhere
on a mountain plateau
that's suspended in air.
There are gargoyles around
that are putrid and faceless
that live on the clouds
just outside
the soul's edge.
The witches abound
and the vultures
seem friendly
till you turn your back on them
and they pluck out your heart.
There's no means of escaping
this Dantesque inferno
it follows you deep
to the well of the brain,
where memories are hidden
and thoughts are forbidden,
where remembering is shunned
for fear of the pain.
This place that I come from
on the mountain plateau
has dangers around
that become incarnations
and tear at your spirit
till you scream and you fall.

This place on the mountain
in the depths of despair
is dressed in foreboding
and will always be with me
to haunt my emotions,
to saddle my hope,
that will never be there.
The only respite
from this den of oblivion
from this curse in my head
and the cross on the wall
will be
death and its shadow,
in its gloom and its glory,
with its sneer and its pomp
when it errantly
comes!

I take refuge

I take refuge
at the top of Mackay and Elmwood,
            looking west and down the hill,
                        where the memories still linger
        and the cotton candy wisdom
        of a younger age
brings uneasy comfort and a sad but bittersweet tranquility.
            Carmen and Gina are on the veranda,
surrounded by the sounds of the ball hockey game,
                that needs to be won
                        to maintain supremacy as
                the street gang
                that affectionately keeps guard
            over all the immigrants of the avenue.
Olga is just coming home from work.
                    I can sense my father,
                            looking at his watch
                    as he sees her strolling
                    down the street
                and really ticked off
                        that she's five minutes late.
            Mother is at the living room window
looking out and pleased,
that her children,
the lifeline to her sanity,
are well and enjoying the warm caress of summertime.
                    It's all a distant haze of shadows
        but I return from time to time,
                    to walk the narrow street and laneway,
                    the bosom of my youth,
to revisit
with the old ghosts,
            in fields of weeds and dreams,
            that are so much a part
                    of what I am,
            today.

It had been one of the best summers

It had been one of the best summers,
    playing in the fields,
listening on the tracks for the train to pass
        and waving at the conductor as if he were
        Horatio on the stern and floating
        through the wide majestic sea.
   The sounds of laughter
still resound
    from those golden days of misspent youth,
oftentimes forgotten,
      that change your life
      for better or for worse,
      who knows?
    But change you do!
        Listening on the tracks for the train to pass
        that day,
        Frankie moved too late!
The sounds of agony still resonate,
from that moment
of golden youth,
     listening on the tracks...
      for the train to pass.

The bell of Santa Maria Delle Grazie

The bell of Santa Maria Delle Grazie
speaks to itself,
unable to touch the people
that pass
alone,
like shadows of flying sparrows.
The old priest is dead,
buried
behind the walls of the old cemetery
that is home to a black moon
and the braying of donkeys
that are unwilling to settle
near the cold,
desolate tombstones
and the rugged road
of tired bodies
and gaunt chestnut trees,
that blossom,
despite the cold and dampness
of the eastern winds.

The midnight breeze

The midnight breeze
  lifts
    the foggy mist
  above the pond
          towards Orion's sad glare
            and the full moon's calm.
  The backdoor light
    serves as home,
          to the insects,
      looking for the rest they get
          when they venture too close
        and their bodies disintegrate against the small hot bulb.
You can hear the frogs,
        intimate old friends,
            calling their lovers,
      in a voice of desperation
            that breaks the eerie quiet of the night.
Open space,
      with nothing but cornstalks,
                lined tall and straight,
                with a look of pride and defiance,
                that will change
  when they hear the sound of the farmer's thrasher
                coming down the road...
The autumn sounds of leaves
        rustling in the trees
untangle my thoughts
        and I can see a thousand years of life
        eroded and left buried in this field.
My mind leans on nothing
  as I gaze at an old rabbit and a turtle
        weeping dewdrops
            near the starlit tufts
                of soft green grass.

It was quiet in the village

It was quiet in the village,
                    late afternoon or so,
          mothers at the river,
                    washing.
You could hear the talk
          and laughter
          and the splashing of the water
as they soaped and rinsed the clothes by hand
and on their knees.
                    No-one worked afternoons,
                         the sun beating down,
                              like uncle Guido's
                         hammer
                    on the red-hot anvil.
          The men sat in the piazza,
          drinking wine,
          playing cards and generally boasting
                    about anything,
               regardless of how trivial,
                              to elevate them
          above
     the mundanities of the long
                    sun ridden days.

Up and down the cobblestone streets
                    young boys played and ran and more often than not
                              could be seen sneaking
                    onto someone's fig tree
                    to steal some fruit and when caught
          being chased away with
                    sonorous and poetic blasphemies
                              at their heels:
"Disgraziati, if I catch you I'm going to beat you with a stick. Wait till I see your mother,
figli di puttana, they took the best figs."
                    Nothing would happen.
          It was almost a mandatory right of passage to be mischievous.
Something
to reminisce about when you got older and sitting in the piazza
drinking wine,
playing 'briscola' and wishing for the smell of the river and the sound of water
                    splashing,
          as the women talk and laugh,
rinsing their clothes,
          by hand
                    and on their knees.

Mimi Sasso

Mimi Sasso era un uomo,
Mimi Sasso was a man,

from the town of Aprigliano
near the catacombs of Hell.

He was tall and indignant
he was elegant and fine,

he could strut
just like a rooster
and his smile could make you blind.

Mimi Sasso era un uomo,
Mimi Sasso was a man,

was adored by all the women
and the men adored him too,

so he galavanted wildly,
his ace was...
no one knew!

He was orphaned by his father
when he was very young
and the only real mother had been
women, wine and song.

Mimi Sasso era un uomo,
Mimi Sasso was a man,

who abused all those who loved him
        raped their psyche
        made them lame,
                        it was narcissistic madness
                                that was fed
                                from mamma's hand,
                                        who herself was far removed
                        from any conscience towards his clan.

        Mimi Sasso era un uomo,
        Mimi Sasso was a man.

Through the years
he grew more conscious
                of his failure as a man
                as a father, as a husband
                        as a neighbour, as a friend.

        Mimi Sasso era un uomo,
        Mimi Sasso was a man,

born to wind and rain and thunder,
        arrogance and sin,
                deep within
                        a well of darkness

                        near the catacombs
                                of Hell.

In her delight

She was already
old and frail
when I saw her
for the first time,
barely four feet tall,
with the light and life
of Venus
on her face.
The black dress
she was wearing
seemed
the perfect setting
for her white hair and anxious smile.
We sat together,
often,
under the shade
of the white mulberry branches,
that had seen
and heard,
more than we could ever talk about.

She reveled in calling me "figliciellù"
while leading me
by the hand,
as if I were still

that little boy
she'd known so long ago,
to the peace and quiet
of the black fig trees
where I played
as a "quatrariellù,"
seeking
what I would
only find,
a few years later
in the
twilight
magic
and the
misty
morning softness
of my daughter's
eyes.

Personality

The rainswept laneway

T. Schiavo – Murdered March 31, 2005

Jasmine

Jack

To Giacomo Leopardi – Poet

Chief Joseph

To Martin Luther King Jr., Assassinated April 4, 1968

To Archbishop Oscar Romero, Assassinated – March 24, 1980

Abercrombie

The rainswept laneway

The rainswept laneway
offered some resistance
to the tip-tap of her
four-inch heels
competing with the tin cans of beer
and garbage on the ground
reflecting broken dreams
and love
that did not last.
Head down,
with nowhere left to go,
her tears reflected
in the neon glaze of sleazy bars and flashing neon lights,
now frozen memories,
hidden,
in the back pocket
of her
faded jeans.

T. Schiavo – Murdered March 31, 2005

She died

amid the jeers and cries

and so did we

and so did

all the prayers we prayed

for justice.

We were diminished on that day,

eroded

to the bone

by courts

and men

indifferent to the

life that died,

that day.

Her life was hers,

was ours,

in those

last days

of folly

and human indiscretion

and so she died,

that day

and so did all the hopes and aspirations

for all

the rest

that twenty thousand years

of deep regret

will not erase,

nor time

forgive,

until

the

end

of

time

because...

she died...

that day.

Jasmine

Jasmine loved her man
but killed him.
His breach of trust
was more than she could bear.
It hurt her deeply
that he loved
another,
her hopes and future
shattered in a day.

She's strong and she'll survive
her sentence,
she has to be
for little Molly's sake
but life's a bitch
there's never any planning,
we only know what is
not what we'll have
and so to all the Jasmines out there,
don't pay no mind
to one low cheatin' man,
it's all the Mollys you cannot forsake,
so don't get
no fool's blood
upon
your hands.

Jack

Jack came,
Jack went.

> The boss hollered,
>> the wife nagged,
>>> the dog bit,
>>>> and the children screamed.
>> Year in and year out,

Jack came,
Jack went.

> It was all he could do that day
> as his legs grew heavier climbing all those stairs,
>>>>> briefcase in hand.
> The thoughts of the noise and the screaming and the pain
>> had become fused and confused until his head rang like a bell.
> He neared the final steps
>> his heart thumped so fast it became a part of his despair.
> He opened the door and stepped onto the roof,
>>> sighed a deep breath and dropped his briefcase,
>> took off his jacket and approached the thin edge of the roof.
> He looked up, closed his eyes, opened his arms, sighed a sigh of relief
and as he felt the rush of air and Heaven filling his lungs and caressing his soul
>> he fell over, onto the street below.
>>>> People paused and then scurried on.
> You could hear someone say: "Oh, well... Jack came... Jack went...!"
> The next day,
>> the boss hollered,
>>> the wife nagged,
>>>> the dog bit,
>>>>> and the children screamed,
> but Jack,
>> Jack was free.

To Giacomo Leopardi – Poet

I took a walk with Giacomo
        late last night
            through fields of wheat and ripe red grapes
                hanging on the vine
which fed the pain and sorrow
of Silvia's last smile.
        Beneath the black fig trees
        he mused
        from time to time
        of how he longed to feel her warm soft hand
            and taste the lips
                that that gave him
                life divine.
        I heard him
        speak
        of love...
      the sweet new style
that recalled troubadours of yore,
whose words caressed his thoughts,
in helping him recall
      the beauty of Silvia's first smile,
      beneath the olive trees
      and golden wheat
      and lonely sparrow
           dancing
           on the vine.

Chief Joseph

Nez Percé Indian Chief
Died 1904 (broken heart)

Head down and broken...
        hell deep in solitude....
                embracing shattered thoughts
                        that hurt
                                remembering the days
of many golden moons
        that brought
        the sun
                and hope
                and mist
        of children dancing in the air
                to this..........
        so far from home
where fresh cold rivers flowed with blood and broken dreams and arrows.
                        He gave his word,
                                they say,
                                        that he would fight,
                                no more,
                                forever,
                        from where the sun set down...
                                        that day...
                                        and cradling
                                the sorrow
                        of a thousand yesteryears
                that mirrored
        in his dark set eyes
        reflecting the mist
                        and clouds
                        and crimson shadows
                                        of lonely wolves
                                and children dancing in the air
                that
        now,
                would be,
        no more.

To Martin Luther King Jr., Assassinated April 4, 1968

He spoke to us of dreams,
the ones he had
while he was young
and grey
and full of time
to dream the hope
that dreamers
dare.
Walking tall that day,
with dream in hand,
he did not know
he would be touching
unborn souls
to dreams he had
that time would not delay!
Who would have known...
and someone did,
that one cold, twirling, nameless piece of steel,
exploding in his heart
would explode millions more
to deep despair.
The shame and sorrow that I felt
could never wash away
my pale
white skin
from off my bones
on that dark day
or since.

To Archbishop Oscar Romero, Assassinated – March 24, 1980

He loved the people in his congregation
he prayed for them
and cried their tears.

He knew they suffered
deep beyond
the hidden places of the soul
where only angels go.

He tried to give them peace and comfort
but you cannot give
what you don't understand,
a brother, father, lover gone forever
no sign of them
in heaven, earth or hell.

Cadavers all about as testimony
the bishops turned around
and walked away.

He tried to get some help
through papal power
but God was gone
that day and did not answer.

The soldiers knew and smiled along the way.
THE GUNS RANG OUT!
Our hearts and his were silenced!
His death,
unjustified,
was justified by courts
and military men that had the sway.

The hopes and aspirations of the people
died with him
on that bloody,
warm March day.

Jimmy Carter prayed before his evening dinner,
Pope John Paul blessed all the world
from his palatial view
and preached for peace and understanding...
then turned around
and walked away...
again...

Abercrombie

Abercrombie was a
spotless image
of
upper crust perfection
as he
sat,
back straight,
ignoring the lights
and silence
and the roar of memories
too vast
to be
remembered
and pulled the trigger
on that cold
black
gun
that took his breath
and drained his
blue blood soul
that was a
spotless image of
upper crust perfection,
encased in silence
and memories
too dark
to be
remembered.

Philosophic Confessions

Hallelujah

I went there

I don't have to talk to you

Sitting on the patio

This Dalian landscape

You are my addiction

I've seen

The Mantra of Merlin-the-Turtle

The sands of time

I know

Hallelujah

Hallelujah, hallelujah
my brother.
Hallelujah, hallelujah
to the wickedness of man.
Hallelujah
my sister,
who wasted her time following man's evil
and who will now perish with him.
Hallelujah, hallelujah,
to a humanity that is not worthy of Eden,
whose eternity
shall now be forfeit.
Hallelujah
to the demi-gods
who were chosen to bring fruit into the world,
who have only spread
their greed
and arrogance
and condemned
billions of lives
to the degeneration
of the soul.
Hallelujah
hallelujah,
they will know my wrath!
When they plead forgiveness
I will trample their souls
within the furthest limits
of oblivion.
Hallelujah, hallelujah
I sent you the prophets of hope
you did not listen.
Hallelujah
was my song to you.

Hallelujah, hallelujah, hallelujah
is now your death bell.
Hallelujah to America,
hallelujah to Germany,
hallelujah to China
hallelujah to Russia,
Hallelujah
to the Rothschilds and the Warburgs,
hallelujah
to the Rockefellers
the Morgans,
the Dulles,
the Stalins
the Bushs
hallelujah to the Monarchy
hallelujah to Charles,
hallelujah
to all the named and unnamed antichrists
who have killed and seduced
millions of people
for their own ends
and that will continue to do so
until every breath
is strangled from them
and they are left to die and rot
on olive trees
and their eyes eaten by harpies.
They have denigrated humanity
and this will not be forgiven
by the angels of mercy.
Hallelujah
to the innocent mothers and children
who were consumed in the genocides
perpetrated by man's inhumanity

for gold, silver
and the beauty of the poppy.
Hallelujah
to the Peruvians,
the Salvadorans,
the South Africans,
the Cambodians
Hallelujah, hallelujah
to all those who have died
unnecessary deaths
since the dawn of man.
Hallelujah
to these innocents,
I will grant the peace and fulfillment of eternity
because they have suffered
too much
for too long.
Hallelujah, hallelujah,
the time is near
when all who have sinned
against the order
of the cosmic sphere
and the universal conscience
will feel the whip upon their spine,
the rod of fire
upon their skin
and the torture of their evil acts
upon their soul.
Hallelujah, hallelujah.
Hallelujah,
was my song to you,
hallelujah, hallelujah,
is now...
your death knoll...

I went there

I went there
yesterday
or was it
yesteryear?
Time stops
and
then
begins,
again,
and ticks a tick
or chimes a chime,
as if,
it
mattered.
We know it
doesn't...
... really!
Yesterday and tomorrow
are only
today
with more conditions,
making it seem,
like time goes by,
only to
come back,
again,
with ticks and chimes,
as if,
it
really
mattered.

I don't have to talk to you

I
DON'T
    have to
        TALK   to you
because

              YOU   don't want to share
yourself
with ME.
           You   only   WANT
   to inflate

             your own ego

        at   MY   expense
and   I   choose
to   DENY   you.
        Your need to
        humiliate me
           is
               YOUR
                  addiction.

Only when YOU learn
     to KNOW me
        through
   my SILENCE
     will I share
          MYSELF
          with
          YOU.

Sitting on the patio

Sitting on the patio of the Café Roma,
sipping on a gin
with
nothing else to do
but watch
the crowds and cars go by.

Thinking only
to get in shape
and when a girl goes by
wondering
if she would look good naked.
I notice a guy,
across the street,
looking at the sky,
not moving,
probably hallucinating,
picturing textural angels
jiving to the beat
of Kelly Jones
jamming
Stereophonic affirmations
that love is blind.
The people walking past him
pretend he doesn't exist because they
scurry by
without making eye contact.

They most likely feel he's a deadhead
who's had too much
to drink
because his wife left him
or he just got ass slapped
with too much taxes
on his workaholic
bullshit
lifestyle ethic
and he's tripping suicidal.
The narratives rush by
so quickly
I need another gin,
just to settle
the straight aesthetic
of my own vision of the view.

This Dalian landscape

This Dalian landscape
buried deep
in my mind,

of hookers on pulpits,
angels on bullets,
demons and clergy
dancing to Bowie,
nudes in the desert
eating mud pies with minstrels
is partly

foreboding,
insight at best
but most certainly
much paranoia.

Images abound
of Hell and high places,
that fly by
with the speed
of American bombs.
I'm trapped by these visions,
the words in the mists,
the shadows of souls
that always remind me.

There's an eternal desire
to get stoned
and to stay there,
to bury my head in the breasts of a goddess,
who will be unnamed,
yet could grant me some comfort.
This tormented existence,
this crippling condition
of fighting the beasts that beat on my brain
is becoming constraining
to the point of exhaustion.
The drums of the Sioux,
the sax of Miles Davis,
the cries of the damned
and the tears of the dead
are often relieving
but becoming perplexing.

I need some relief
from this labyrinth of damnation,
to find some good hash
or get nailed to a cross.

You are my addiction

You
    ARE
            my addiction.
    The trans-angelic angel
                of my thoughts
    and
        keeper of my quiet
        desperation.
You
    ARE
        my need.
The guide
        that cools the
    everlasting flames
of hopeless inspiration.

I've seen

I've seen the other side
        of rising sunsets
                and felt the darkness
                        on my lover's lips.

I've been through clouds
        on magic carpets
                somewhere
                        but I've never seen
                the other side of Hell.

I've seen the other side
        of midnight madness
        between despair
                and magic mushroom visions,

    lost time
    on roads
        that never
        should be taken,
                yet I've never seen
                        the other side
                        of pain.

I've seen the other side
        of truth and beauty,
        slept with hookers
                on cold dark streets
and lonely,
park-side avenues,
        hallucinated vestal virgins
                in a crystal palace,
    but I've never seen
            the other side
            of me.

The Mantra of Merlin-the-Turtle

I have seen the world forever
in all its incarnations,
felt the wind and cold and fire
since before the dawn of man.

I have seen the death of dinosaurs,
the destruction of the Ice Age,
the battle scars of Vishnu,
the plight of the Lakota.

I am slow
the earth is patient
and there is nowhere to go.
I have learned that love is better
than the need to wage a war.

I have lived a life of peace,
I have shared my space with all,
from the deserts in New Mexico
to the mountains of Nepal.

I have witnessed the upheavals
of all creatures since their birth,
followed man from simple caves
to his dominion of the earth.

One thing I've learned for certain
as I've journeyed to and fro,
man's greed and need to conquer
will destroy the world I know.

The sands of time

The sands of time
                brushed softly
                on my brow
                                today
                                as
                warming rays
                of morning sunshine
                caressed
        that sad and serious strain
    of mildly
    dignified
    sensitivity
                        that
    too many days and years
                of lost hopes
                            have mercilessly eroded.
    The magic moments have
                                dissipated.
The dedication
        to norms and convention
                        has been given
            a sad ending.

The usually
        artful and balanced psyche
                has become a fragile
                    and complexly fermented
        cesspool
           of the most
    unmitigated
        torment.
The sands of time
        brush softly
on my mind,
        reminding me
           that the important moments
           be remembered
    and that
        the long
    black shadows
    of doubt
    and self-absorption
        be buried
        and left
        forgotten,
    deep beneath,
    the sands of time.

I know

I know you are coming
I know you are Death.
Just give me
a second,
I must take a breath.
  I'm reliving some memories
   of the things
    in my past,
of the laughter and tears
and the days
that don't last.
     Hold on
    one more moment
    I know I must go,
let me just feel the love
that I felt
long ago,
for lovers and friends
and others I knew
and those that were honest,
loyal and true.
   Just tarry a while
    I know you can wait
     I must resolve some issues,
      I must
       get them straight.

Don't come any closer,
            just listen oh Death!
                        I'll give you my life,
                                    I will not give my breath.

Recalling my years is taking much longer,
than moments or seconds
and I'm growing much stronger
                        and just so you know,
                        I will no longer plead,
                        I will take the hours
                                    and days that I need.

My life is my own,
it's my gift to keep,
to share it with those
that I choose.............
                        so please take my heed.
                                    I'm glad that you came
                                                but now you must go
                                    and if I ever need you,
                                                you'll be...
                                    the last one....... to know.

Reflections

Western landscapes

The screams the shouts

The curtain

Special occasions

Mix up the party

Turn the television off

It's just another day

It had been a battle

Garden delights

Explain the hoaxes

Additional engines

We're on the dark side of the moon

They strode

There are no angels in Heaven

Foreign affairs

Eden in a pill

A place in the sun

Western landscapes

Western landscapes
        banging billboards
    over sunlit moons and laneways
                    filled with merchants
        torn from heaven
        near some eastern Shanghai villas
                    selling twisted rusty tin cans
        clanging psychedelic solos
        on the frozen legs of winos
                    clutching pages from the Times
    that sells diets made in South Beach
        near the palaces of the crac heads
        wearing silk ties
    drinking whiskey
        from the breasts of lonely hookers
    lost forever in the shadows
    of their father's mid-east vision
                    in the land of lost horizons
        that was home
    once
        on the range
    to Mickey Mantle
and the "coolies"
    laying tracks for North Pacific with
    the martyrs of Hells Kitchen
    sitting jobless
        in the bars
        of lanky mobsters that were heartless
but now dead
and doing service
in the presence of the Lord.

The screams the shouts

The screams
the shouts,

the innocent
torn from their straw beds
shadows of their former selves,
the skeletons of a world gone mad.

The screams
the shouts,

thrown into the darkness of their souls
to be offered as sacrifices
to the litany of the fallen angels.

The screams
the shouts,

of mothers lamenting their headless children
and husbands hanging lifeless
on the branches of the tree of guilt
and hate
and hopeless futures.

The screams
the shouts

of the Jew
the Kurd
the Armenian
the Rwandan
the women and girls of Sierra Leone
raped and sodomized
with their limbs hacked off
because

the screams
the shouts,

do not reach our humanity
or are nullified
by the coke that we must drink
and the cars that we must drive.

The shouts
the screams,

that the Wailing Wall becry,
that the Bible, the Torah and the Quran
drown out
and that only serve to increase

the screams
the shouts

of pain and torture and mutilation
that have been heaped upon mankind

by the self-rightous,
shameless leaders of our tribes.

The screams
the shouts,

reach out
to the future generations
that will be born into servitude,
hunger
and the degradation
of the body and the spirit.

The screams
the shouts,

cry out for the justice
of the universal order
and it will come to pass
because cherubs do fly
and there are fires in Hell that await those that inflict
the screams,
the shouts,
that our minds should not erase
because they touch the soul of EVERYMAN (anon).
The screams
the shouts,
the screams
the shouts,
from the screams
the shouts,
may we all be delivered
on a Sunday afternoon,
at press time,
just before the start of the Super Bowl.

The curtain

The curtain is opening,
Oz is exposed,
Valhalla is no longer enchanted.
We see
darkness is falling
on our
deceptive pink vision
and cave art
tells us no lies.
We spin from the shock
as we tumble from grace
and we see
the deception
quite clearly.
The passion of Jesus
helps to sanctify H-bombs
and therapy
serves
as the devil's only
disguise.
The enigma
is turning
all angels to aliens,
Wall Street
sells strategies
for what bankers,
and presidents,
drug lords and
popes
will allow you to know.

I need to get loaded,
I'm losing perspective,
losing hope of redemption,
when lunacy
serves
as the wisdom
of David and Saul.

Popular myths, religion and culture
become digital shadows
on high-speed PC's,
sin and contrition
have become one and the same,
the Egos
are fighting
the Ids
for acceptance
with consciousness
suffering
a slow painful death.

The curtain has opened,
Oz was a fake,
the mirror is shattered,
the vultures are circling,
Jefferson's words
are lost in Biloxi,
salvation is found in a bottle of Rye
and you know that
we're screwed
because astronomers
hide out
in Manhattan.

Special occasions

Special occasions
              are there all around us
elaborate lies
              that dictate existence.
Long-term
       marriages
              are measured
              in months
                        only the vows in the church,
                        last a lifetime.
       Christmas is fleeting
              in its promise
                     of peace,
                            GOODWILL
                     is a verbal abstraction,
                     a meaningless gesture
                     to the thousands of poor,
                            that starve and die
                     in Manila,
                            but my reason
                                   to wrap up your gift.
       Pilgrims
              on a march
              to Mecca,
              for Islam,
              will kindly blow up
                            a school bus
                            in Haifa
                     and the Pope
                     condemns condoms in Niger.

Special occasions
    are fun and distracting
        lived in the mind
        as delusion,
                formal affairs
                that give reason
          for living
                  because reality
                      just isn't fair!
        it wakes up our senses,
      tests our compassion,
      humanity is not our affair!
Special occasions,
     like mass
     on a Sunday,
     who needs the poor and the lame?

Mix up the party

Mix up the party
with pornography stars
then have a coke
with Easter egg salad and Honduran cigars
on the side.

There's Castro and Eastwood
offering
insane
perspectives
on rules
that never applied.

Socialites dancing
to jazz and the waltz
with black and white tears
and a touch of pimento
on their
virgin
Versacci
gowns.

The directors are looking
at Mrs. Moore's
buttocks
while Peter Pan's
locked up
in jail,
eating ice cream and donuts,
sushi and fries,
applying
dollar store
make-up
and spreading
obscene little lies.

                                    Veggie spaghetti
                              for civil war lackeys
                        who shot dogs
                  on the way to El Paso.
                        They're tired and bloody
                  ticked off and hungry

                              and it seems
                              like they really
                                    don't care.

      Greek gods like Brad
                  ride emergency cars
                              over Cosby's
                                    layaway girlfriends

            and
the early arrivers
            get Halloween treats
                  from a
                        sumptuous Jolie
                              who's
                        as fresh as a strawberry sundae.
                              The British attractions
                        are off doing dope
                  in a bathroom
                              that's covered with breath mints
                  and all they can see
                  while they're roasting
                              like almonds
                  are turbines where icicles hang.

Mix up the party
with "Deppian" doubles
Pavarotti
is wailing
his favourite tunes
and Miss Rivers
is down
on her knees.
Childbearing playgirls
are topless and tight
and some madonna is sucking
on leg bone caffeine
oozing sex
for a two dollar fee.

Mix up the party,
the sultan is waiting,
the show is about to begin.
Pull up a chair,
the cards have been dealt
and the auction
is just
ringing
in.

Turn the television off

Turn the television off.
Stop reading the news.
To hell with news magazines.
I'm going back on hash.
I need to get high.
I can't stand my neighbour
who's doing
my girlfriend.
I'm being forced
into believing
that Arabs
want to blow up our petunias
and our garages and our damned mini-vans.
When was it that we lost our ability to think?
When
did the manipulation
begin?
I need a dose of Deepak in a tube, it relaxes you
and opens your consciousness
to the wonders of the world.
I need to make sense of this mess,
I need to be ticked off and enjoy it.
We need a new incarnation.
I've lost all my heroes,
Spiderman used to be fine,
now
he's dating a girl.
Marco called me
a fundamentalist Christian-Muslim, beer-drinking, wise guy.
Aaaaauuuuugggggghhhhh,
doesn't he know
I'm a conservative
but slightly reformed pseudo-Italian
working in Woodbridge
and I love redheads

but I married a blonde?
Okay so he was right!
That is the cause of my neurosis,
my blonde wife who's uncritical
but gay.
I don't want to offend Canadians
but they're virtual rednecks.
There's no hockey on Saturday night
so I'm screwed.
I can only keep my thumb
up my tweezer
for so long... eh!
I have better things to do
than move my sofa
and think about who my grandchildren
are going to look like in thirty years.
I need some advice,
I need Opra when she's not dieting.
She's easier to talk to
when she's not busy
with world affairs.
The crucifixion was bogus
but Jesus walked on water
and I heard he loved donkeys.
Are you getting the picture,
or did Martha go to jail in vain?
There is no
historical imperative
that we be correct.
Mary Magdalene could have been a virgin,
she knew some of the right moves.
I read it in the Vatican Sun,
in an article next to the Pope
who was smiling.
You'll make more sense if you tweak,

ask the Chinese in their opium dens but I'm sure the English won't believe them.
I met a neurotic Jew
who told me
Buddha lives in Brooklyn,
Martha agrees and she's connected to Vinnie who's connected to Guido.
Nixon hated them all,
equally
and he's no longer connected.
There IS FAIRNESS IN THE LAND!
I need social validation
even though
the Bible is melting the Canadian north,
killing
the South Americans
and infecting the Africans with AIDS.
If you don't believe this
ask a Haitian!
Don't go away
we'll be back in a minute.
Trudeau was a commie.
We all loved his million-dollar home
and Gucci condoms.
BUTT Barbara is not talking
and
that's as good as it gets.
I may go to Hell
but God won't allow it
because of the irreducible complexity theory,
Behe is no fool
and I still need to get laid
in the wasteland
that's my mind.
Take 2
Cut to commercial!

It's just another day

It's just another day
in eastern Pickwick,
the ferry's gone
and I'm left all alone.
The mail is late again
my fridge is empty
and fire engine sounds
unleash my pain.

It's just another day
in Oklahoma
where tragedy takes on
a different face,
the prayers they pray
are never really answered
but they're sure
their souls were
in a state of grace.

It's just another day
in southern Cape Town,
the body count
has risen by a score,
the AIDS is killing
by the thousands,
it's worse
by far
than any senseless war.

It's just another day
in my mind's memory,
when things were
simpler than they are today,
when children smiled
and played together,
before the world
just carried them away.

It had been a battle

It had been a battle,
fighting the snow,
trees
and jagged rocks of that mountainside.

Only the warm sun and adrenaline rush of blood sustained him
to this moment...

With its face and eyes in sight
he dared not move
but he could smell 'the kill.'
Any noise would scare away this trophy.
He looked at it,
still and quiet,
unable to breathe,
frozen in time,
each second an hour.
As he steadied his aim and gazed deeper into its eyes
he became fascinated by a look that reflected satin
softness and the wisdom and knowledge of the ages,
touched by a compassion
that no man could ever comprehend.

He stood shaken!
He had connected with the soul and heart of the beast,
touched its thoughts.
As he drifted into the consciousness of his spirit
he pulled the trigger.

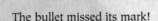

The bullet missed its mark!

It took a moment for him to drop his rifle
as he stood frozen in time,
each second a day.
He gazed at the mountaintop
sitting far into the afternoon stillness of the sky

and feeling his blood rush and his spirits soar
at having felt the hand of God,
through those woven eyes,
he turned and walked away,
carrying with him the wonders of the majesty of the universe
and a new love,

that no man
should fail
to understand.

Garden delights

Garden delights

      of fresh fruits
       and flowers
   all sit quite stylish
    with their

          seasonal touches.

   Hand painted cakes
   are covered with roses
and all other kinds
of new twists and flavours.

         These are trendy new ways

   to express
   devotion

     to very engrossing
   and irrelevant notions.

With napalm
  being dropped
on a country or two

        we savour the pastries
        that are coloured in blue

and the buttercream frosting
that's actual magic

    was whipped up
    in Laos
     on the back
      of a child.

We should all
take great pleasure
in this wonderful fare

     but let's
      not
      go about
       with our nose
     in the air.

Explain the hoaxes

Explain the hoaxes
let them unravel,
look deeper... into the stories you read.
The bankers on Wall Street
WANT YOU
to fear,
it's a surefire way
of getting control.
Is legend science
or science unreal?
Try being a skeptic
it will all be revealed.
When something big happens,
ask "whom does it serve?"
You'll be surprised at what you will learn.

They need deception
it's their tool for survival,
Pascal was right
we all can be fooled.
Did man land on the moon
or a back lot in Phoenix?
Was Kennedy killed by one man or twenty?
The War of the Worlds was really a warning,
Agent Orange and Anthrax can't be escaped.
What's fake and what's real?
Can you explain?
Should I or shouldn't I trust the people I trust?
Was it really Bin Laden
that blew up the towers,
are we getting a clear view
of foreign affairs?
We're told this and that about this and the other
then we find out
it was bullshit at best.
Explain the hoax,
ask the Federal Reserve,
the Bank of Canada won't fare any better,
credit card companies launder money for druglords,
interest rates on them keep people enslaved.
When public utilities start going private
pack up your bags and move to Nantucket.
The script that's being written,
for man
by his master,
is far more insidious than a Christ on the cross.

The truth or a hoax?
Let it unravel,
look very closely... at what you think... you believe.

Additional engines

Additional engines that watch all Bangkok natives,
small writing tools for Columbian drug lords,
                        G.I. Joe targets
                        asleep in the Gulf,
            calico carpets for my Tennessee home.
The slapstick is real
                that guards Quaker ambitions
                and barn buildings burn
                as M.o.n.s.a.n.t.o. glides by.
New cars and affluence
are a passing tradition
a craze that's gone south
for the American child.
                        Women seek titles
                        a pig knows its place
                and Middle East cowboys
                dance
                on Arlington graves.

        Smoke a tinsel cigar
                while New York is burning
                                with Bullwinkle mooning
                        the English tsarina
who's holed up in Jersey under Palisades Park.

James Bond has dodged
 an Egyptian eye symbol
   that shows up quite clearly
  on a ten dollar bill,
 so switch your position,
  strange things are happening
 take back the purchases and turn on the lights,
   it's time to take action,
   it's time for resolve,
   it's time for a Colt,
  to halt the disease.

Measure your footsteps
wash off all the chemtrails
smile to your neighbour
  and steer clear of Chicago.

We're on the dark side of the moon

We're on the dark side of the moon
>> and falling.

We're on the dark side of the moon
>> and falling fast.

When we give up
>> our tomorrows
>>> for the sake
>>>> of yesterday,

when we fail to see the signs
>> that are strewn along our way,

> then,

we're on the dark side of the moon
>> and falling.

We're on the dark side of the moon
>> and falling fast.

Malcom X should still be here
>> and talking.

Martin Luther should be
>> living out his dream.

John Lennon's song
>> was ended
>>> much too soon
>>>> so just... imagine!

We're on the dark side of the moon
>> and falling.

We're on the dark side of the moon
>> and falling fast.

Gandhi was a man for all the ages,

Mandela fights the fight
>> and carries on believing
>>> but the AIDS
>>>> has killed his dreams
>>>>> and life's no better...

Romero's world of justice
　　　　　was over
　　　　　　　　in a second
　　　　　　　　　　　but not before John Paul was
　　　　　　　　　　　　　　　seen in Hell.
We're on the dark side of the moon
　　　　　　　　and falling.
We're on the dark side of the moon
　　　　　　　　and falling fast.

Kissinger
　　　　made
　　　　　　　Pol Pot a hero.
　　　　　　　　Three million dead
　　　　　　　　　　and so who gives a damn?

George keeps killing
　　　　　where he wants to:
　　　　　　　　　Afghanistan, Iraq and next Iran.
　　　　　　　　　　He lied and said it was for freedom
　　　　　　　　　　but it's the drug and bank cartels
　　　　　　　　　　he's pleasing.

We're on the dark side of the moon
　　　　　　　　and falling.
We're on the dark side of the moon
　　　　　　　　and falling fast.
Mother Trisa was a fake and we can prove it.
O.J. did the crime and we all know.
Waco didn't have to happen
　　　　　　but we've come to realize
　　　　　　　　　　the files
　　　　　　　　　　　　just had to go.

Was Princess Di killed

        for cavorting

            with an Arab?

                Did Charles have a hand in Enron too?

We're on the dark side of the moon

           and falling.

We're on the dark side of the moon

           and falling fast.

The multinationals

        are turning us

        into mindless zombies

the freedoms that we thought we had are gone.

The conspirators are coming out for

             world dominion,

             so we better learn to read those signs

             and read them now.

We're on the dark side of the moon

           and falling.

We're on the dark side of the moon

          and

           f

             a

              l

               l

                i

                  n

                   g

                       fast.

They strode

They strode
forward
bravely,
sincerely,
without hesitation.
They believed
the "liar and the father of lies,"
his flawless ability to
victimize and divide.
They strode forward
and died.
Helpless fools
in their sincerity,
in their innocence,
in their last
moment
of glory.
In the land
of Nod.

There are no angels in Heaven

There are no angels in Heaven
only wise guys in limos
turning tricks for a beer and a dance.
The saints are all marching to Tupac
while harlots from Jarvis
do cops
who were vicious
and limp.
The crac heads
that died
in stinking dark stairways
overdosing
from total indifference
supplied by the rich and well-bred,
are off planting flowers,
in high-priced silk coffins,
that Mary
puts on her head.
Children who died in abortions
are feeding their mothers
who are locked
in a fetal position.
They ooze blood
and some tears
from the sores made of pain
but mostly the guilt
they must bear.

The landlords
that threw out their tenants,
that worked hard but just couldn't pay,
the soldiers that fired their guns
for the thrill of watching
men die,

        the politicians that lied,
        the priests that broke trust,
        the popes that killed with their silence,
        are now doing time

                near the house of the Lord,
                   who's spreading His arms
                with the liberals and bankers
           being welcomed with love and compassion.
The angels are watching,
        with a look of repulsion
        as they
        fly off to Dallas
scratching their heads on the way.

Foreign affairs

Foreign affairs
or getting laid on a Monday?

What are my choices
for my fear of death?

Was Baghdad for oil
or the future of Islam?
Is p.h.i.z.e.r distracting
my view of Sudan?

Argentina's collapse
is tied
to the war
in Rwanda
the AIDS crisis
checks all the African states.

Rescuing refugees
is public diplomacy
we need
Polish hookers on our streets and our bars.

Foreign affairs
or porn star erotica?
What are the
choices
for my fear of death?

Eden in a pill

Eden in a pill,
the sustainer
of life,
the healer
of mankind,
it's important,
it's paramount,
it's so hard to find.
Enjoy the adventure,
it won't last
too long,
then you'll need
another
but a little more
strong.
Lose yourself,
be willing
to follow,
go into a trance,
it will surely assist you,
in being robotic,
in being real shallow.
Give in
to p.h.i.z.e.r. get an erection
it's sexy,
it's sensual
and simply in style.

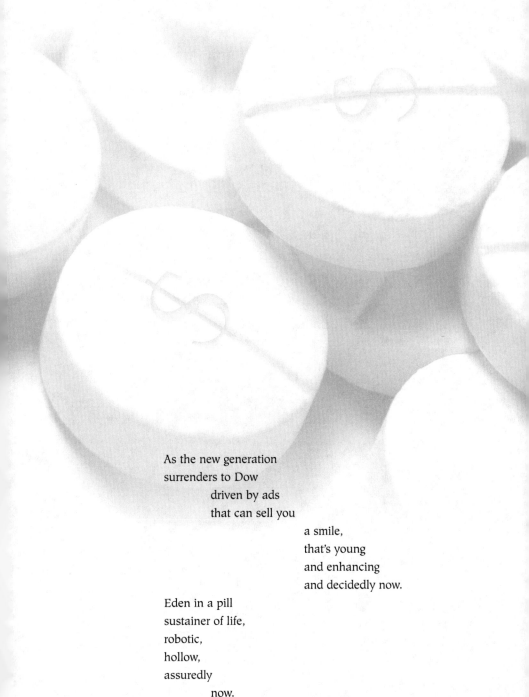

As the new generation
surrenders to Dow
    driven by ads
    that can sell you

                a smile,
                that's young
                and enhancing
                and decidedly now.

Eden in a pill
sustainer of life,
robotic,
hollow,
assuredly
      now.

A place in the sun

A place in the sun.
    A child out of wedlock
        behaviour most frequently noted.
    A natural response
    to blue crystals,
      ritual is a dying tradition.

White linen napkins,
    purple green chairs
      and daytime affairs
        that dazzle the senses.
    Classic
    fresh options,
      a theory debunked,
    the high price of whiskey
      and dinner at GiGi's on Friday.

When you look at the picture
what is it you see?
    That your car can be fun
      but it isn't a Jag?
    That caviar sucks?
    or you don't need
      The music
        of Prince?

Love

You said

There is a lovely lilac tree

The loving in your eyes

The ladies

Since you've been gone

She called me

I felt your heartbeat

I stepped into the parlour

I looked into your eyes

I danced with the gypsies

He just wanted a light

Aurora Borealis

I will remember you

You said

You said you would be
    here...
                ... today
just like yesterday,
    while
    I
    waited,
    head down,
    for time to pass,
enduring wrenching silence
    in a pain that
only Atlas
    could endure
and yet,
I'll wait,
again
              and then some more
              and hope THAT hope
    just as I did yesterday,
head down,
enduring pain
in wrenching silence
and waiting
once again,
for time
to make up time
    and then
        to pass.

There is a lovely lilac tree

There is a lovely lilac tree
     outside my window,
          near the stairs,
whose fragrance fills my senses,
with daylight thoughts
of you
and simmering summer nights.

          The blush rose of its blossoms,
               mingled
                    with its mint-green leaves,
          is not ignored,
     by the hummingbird and robins,
               that shuttle to and fro,
                    from branch to branch,
                         marvelling
                    at the wisdom
               of its naked beauty.

          Crickets,
     near the fallen flowers,
          make joyful noises and let their passions run free,
          unashamed,
     as they rustle
          between the sunlight
               and their lover's smile.

The loving in your eyes

The loving in your eyes
                        has faded.

        It's gone from golden red
                to cold despair.

    I knew
                I'd seen it leave
some time forever,

                when summers waned
        and midnights
                grew
                        too long.

    I still can hear you
                whisper softly.
                        I feel your ruby breath
                        upon my skin.

            But something tells me I am
        only dreaming,

    It's time to say
                goodbye
                        and bid
                                farewell.

The ladies

The ladies all looked
gallant in their wardrobes,
                        from dazzling pink
                        to scarlet red
and deep-set shades
of burgundy and blue
            and all the while their smiles
                        were
plastic moldings and their gait was one of...
                "hey you... never
                        mind."

The bodies they had on
were trim perfection
that could
seduce
at will
most any man,

                their hair
                    was silk and radiant in the
                                    distance,
        the pearls and diamonds caused a golden glare
                and when the show was over...
done...
completed,
                we went back home half stoned without a care
but then we wake up feeling sick but sober
                                no gallant ladies and no plastic smiles.
            We make a promise we will not revisit
but we do because we're products
                        of our lies...

Since you've been gone

Since you've been gone
I no longer sit by the window,
absorbing the warmth
of the early morning sun
that kept me close to you.
The doors are locked,
the curtains are all drawn.
The odd ladybug
that finds its way
onto my shirt sleeve
is all the company I need.
We smile
gently
at each other,
a knowing smile,
that reduces the frantic cries
that only we can hear
within our deepest thoughts,
whose past is gone
and have no witness for tomorrow.
The bitterness of lonely days
stings with an endless zeal
and all my hopes
evaporate to dusk

and wither
just to die.

She called me

She called me,

again,

last night

or this morning.

I can't remember.

I was too strung out

with nauseous

memory loss

caused by overzealous

dedication

to vodka's ability

to numb the senses

and rot the brain

to the point of breathlessness

and indifference

to the world

and anyone in it.

That is not to say

that I give a damn

when I'm half sober.

I am normally filled with disgust and loathing
                    for myself and for
                    everyone around me
                    even on a good day.
                              I block out the tune of multimedia
                    corporate
                    political bullshit hype
                              that addicts don't matter...
                                        but they do!

So to hell
with the tedious
mundane
senseless
superficial
inanities
of the world.
          If it doesn't come out of a bottle and it isn't 80 proof
                    it's not worth it.

I felt your heartbeat

I felt your
    heartbeat
    once
        and then
        again
and looked
into
your eyes...
    ... just... once!
    It wasn't long
    and not
      so long
      ago
but still my thoughts
    and yours
    united us...

just once...
and not for long
and not
so long
ago.

I stepped into the parlour

I stepped into the parlour
  one more time,
to drink the perfume in the air
   and take a sip of your pure brandy wine.
  The time was short
   but bittersweet and fine,
      enough to fill the senses in my mind.
I'll raise a toast,
I'll close my eyes
and taste the soft wet dew between your thighs
    just one more time,
   to make it real,
   to make it last,
   to make it feel eternal...
       one more time.

I looked into your eyes

I looked into your eyes
          that day
          and loved you.
                    You didn't know it
          then
                    but you do now.
          I still can hear your voice
                    caress my heart_____
          you gave me peace
     and made me feel secure.
                    You look into my eyes
                         again,
          I feel your love,
     I didn't know it then
                    but I do now.

I danced with the gypsies

I danced with the gypsies,
                    spoke to the fools,
          wasted my time
     reading Chaucer.

     I killed my best friend
               with kindness and trust,
was given repose by a stranger.

               Laid down with the harlots,
                         confessed to my god,
          who was busy with Stalin at dinner.

     Visiting Hell was
               too much like praying
but the hash gave me freedom
               from pain.
                    I looked in your eyes
                         as you looked into mine,
          felt a long peace and comfort
          for once in my life
          and shed
                    for all time
          my strong fear...
                         of dying.

He just wanted a light

He just
wanted
a light

        not

             her life story

                 but he

                    went

                        to her room
                        just the same.

From a smoke

        to some brandy

and a whiskey or two

                she was ready
                to give him

                        a wink.

Not since the 23rd hour

           of any good day
           had he

              gotten

                so much

                    for so little.

      A comfy old bed,
         a night
         of pure
         rapture,
         it just doesn't get

                any
                better.

Aurora Borealis

Aurora Borealis
                take my heart,
                        to the
        furthest regions
                        of the Northern Lights,
                to that place
                        of ice and snow
                                where
                we know
                the sun
                        will never rise.

Aurorea Borealis
                        be my guide,
                keep me
                from this life of pain,
                        this life of strife.
                        She is gone
                        and won't be back
                        but your amber lights
                will lead me on
                with soft
                        illuminated
                pink blue
                        flares
                        of seamless hope.

Aurora Borealis
keep my heart,
shed the light and splendour
of your radiance
that inspires
flickering rays
of faith
to all mankind.
Aurora Borealis
please reach out,
beyond the endless
sphere of soft blue
landscapes
draping over
boundless
shapeless nights that touch that inner part of me that is no more.
Let me ride your mystic clouds
let my spirits rage
forever
in the curtains of the dancing lights
and glittering vastness
of the bright
pulsating
flames of twirling red green visions of the evening sky.
Aurora Borealis
hear my heart,
let my breath
be still
and let the resonance
of all your colours
fill my soul,
since she is gone
and won't
be back
again!

I will remember you

I will remember you,
my golden goddess of another time,
my muse,
my sweet desire,
that tenderly embraced
the yearnings in my soul.

I will remember you
through days of drought
and endless cold dark nights
when I'm alone
and all the bright lights in my spirit wane.

I will remember you
when my thoughts linger
to those tender moments,
in a place,
that only we would share.

I will remember you
and smile
and taste the fragrance of your soft white skin
once more,
just to remember you,
my muse,
my inspiration
of another time.

Don't Miss

Murder in the Piazza

A story you won't be able to put down...

By

R. Gallucci

Gallucci was born in Aprigliano (Cosenza), Italy,
but has lived in Canada since 1954. He received
his Honours BA at the University of Toronto, and
his BEd from Teachers College.

www.mimisasso.com